AUDREY O'DONOHUE

Audrey

WISE WORDS FOR A LIFE OF MEANING

Published by Enlightenment Publishing

in partnership with Influence Publishing Inc., June 2022

ISBN: 978-0-6454636-2-0

Copyright © 2022 by Audrey O'Donohue

All rights reserved. No part of this publication may be reproduced, stored in or introduced into a retrieval system, or transmitted, in any form, or by any means (electronic, mechanical, photocopying, recording or otherwise) without the prior written permission of the publisher. This book is sold subject to the condition that it shall not, by way of trade or otherwise, be lent, resold, hired out, or otherwise circulated without the publisher's prior consent in any form of binding or cover other than that in which it is published and without a similar condition including this condition being imposed on the subsequent purchaser.

Developmental Editor: Natalie Brown

Cover Design & Illustrations: Cristina Londono

Typesetting: Tara Eymundson

DISCLAIMER: Readers of this publication agree that neither Audrey O'Donohue, nor her agent, nor her publisher will be held responsible or liable for damages that may be alleged as resulting directly or indirectly from the use of this publication. Neither the publisher, nor the agent, nor the author can be held accountable for the information provided by, or actions resulting from, accessing these resources.

ACKNOWLEDGEMENTS

To Natalie, my agent and my friend:
Thank you for all you have done.
Thank you for what you are about to do!
But most of all, thank you for being you!

With thanks to Cristina Londono at Wallnut Studio
for providing the beautiful illustrations for this book.

The following quotations and sayings are a collection from the author or extracted from

A Life of Enlightenment Volume 1: The Journey of an Extraordinary Woman.

Other sources are quoted when it is not the original work of the author.

This is a book of wisdom.
Enjoy.

Love

Audrey

These sayings are to point your nose.
It is up to you to sniff.

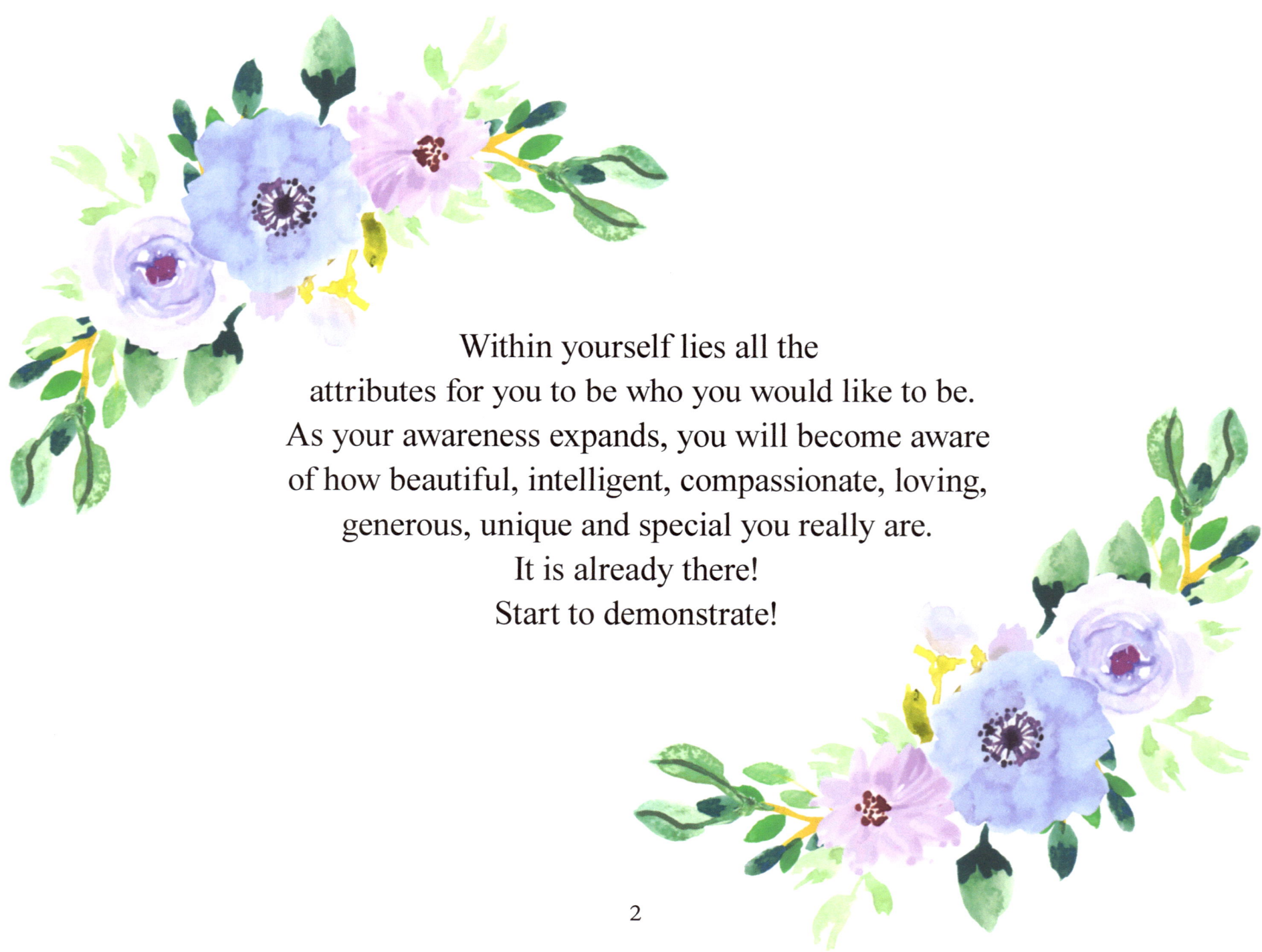

Within yourself lies all the
attributes for you to be who you would like to be.
As your awareness expands, you will become aware
of how beautiful, intelligent, compassionate, loving,
generous, unique and special you really are.
It is already there!
Start to demonstrate!

Courage is rightly esteemed the best of all human qualities because it is the quality which guarantees all others.

—*paraphrased quote from Aristotle*

You do not have a soul.
It is not something you carry around like a suitcase.
YOU ARE A SOUL.

How do you describe a being?
Words are inadequate.
The closest I can say is that a being is a nothingness
with the potential of everythingness.

Always grant another beingness.

There is beingness, but man believes there is only becomingness.

You only recognise in another those qualities, virtues or issues that you yourself hold.

A being's basic ability is to make something out of nothing or nothing out of something.

If you were the only person on earth, you would have no idea who you really were.

All the tools that you use,
whether they be cards, crystals, mediums or clairvoyants,
serve as permission slips to assist you to be who you truly are.

You are already an expert at manifesting.
What do you think got you to where you are today?

Worried about the outcome of an event?
Look ahead twenty-four hours and see and relish its success.

You create your own reality.

You are your own happiness.

You are your own serenity.

You create and/or co-create your own reality.
Nothing can happen to you without your presence.
Your presence is always your choice.

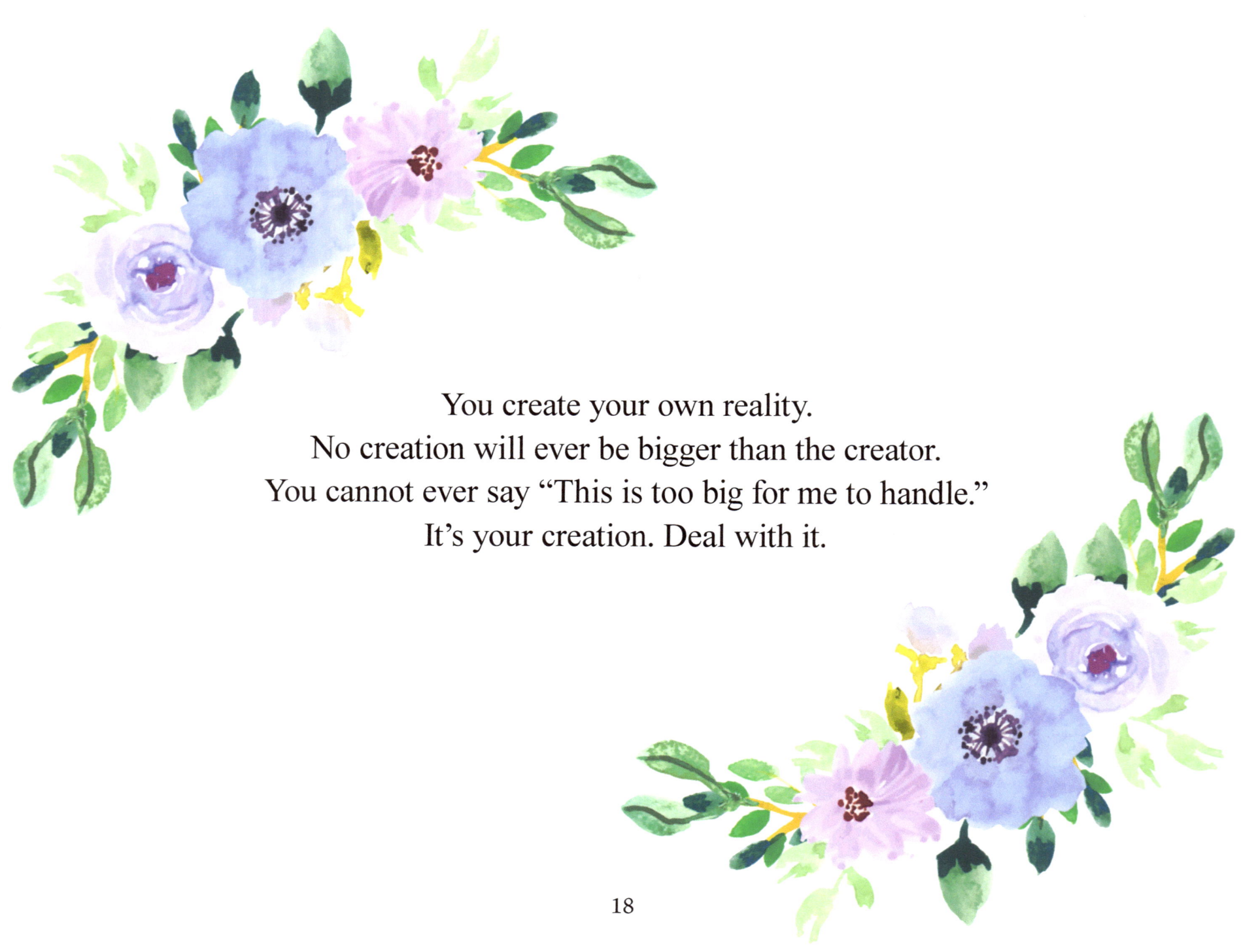

You create your own reality.
No creation will ever be bigger than the creator.
You cannot ever say "This is too big for me to handle."
It's your creation. Deal with it.

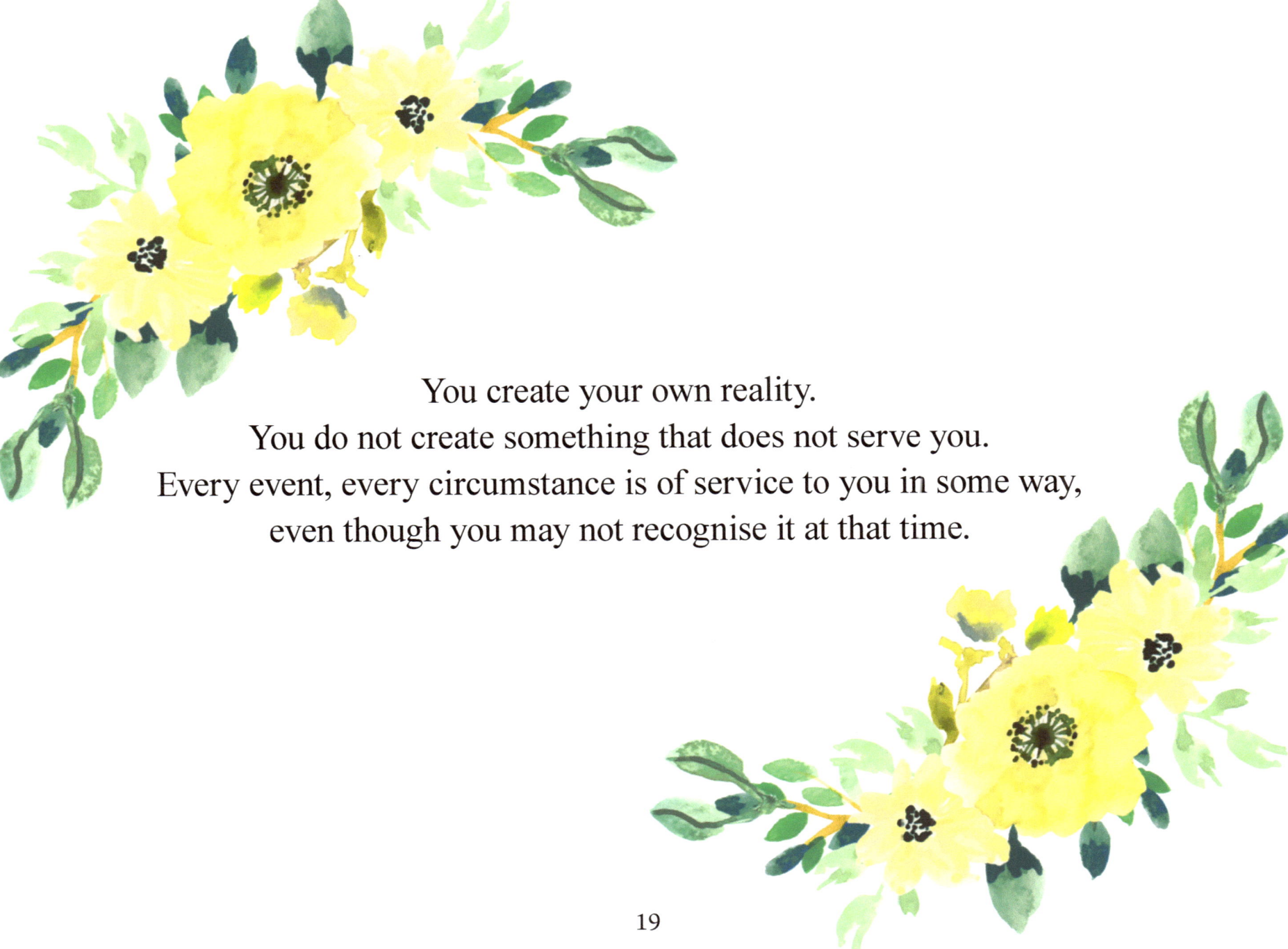

You create your own reality.
You do not create something that does not serve you.
Every event, every circumstance is of service to you in some way,
even though you may not recognise it at that time.

You are here to have an effect on your life.
You are your life!
Life is not meant to have an effect on you!

Abundance:
The ability to do what you need to do when you need to do it.
It isn't necessarily money, but it can be.

Expansion is a product of inclusion, not exclusion.

When you are at the top,
that is really the beginning of the next level.

Most thinking is wandering in condensed spaces.

The most important priority in your life
is your own personal growth.

Resistance always creates conflict.
No resistance is acceptance. Acceptance puts you at Cause.
Resistance puts you at Effect.
Acceptance and allowing creates peace and growth.

Every event whether positive or negative
contributes to your growth if you allow it.
Your allowance dictates your expansion as a being.

A habit is an unknowingness. Once you KNOW, it is a choice.
When you spot the exact habit…it is handled.

Everything is perfect.
When you don't get what you want, it is wise to want what you get.
You always create your own reality.

You have to make all these new things a habit; so it is just a matter of doing them until you don't have to think of them anymore.

If you want to be enlightened, then be willing to lighten up.

Circumstances do not dictate your state of being.
Your state of being dictates circumstances.

For what purpose?
A good question for almost every circumstance or action
where you have even a slight doubt.

Everything that happens;
all the events in your life, serve you in some way.
It may not be apparent at the time,
but it will be in the near future.

Assign positive meanings
to everything that happens to you.
This allows you to stay in touch and work with
your Divine higher self.

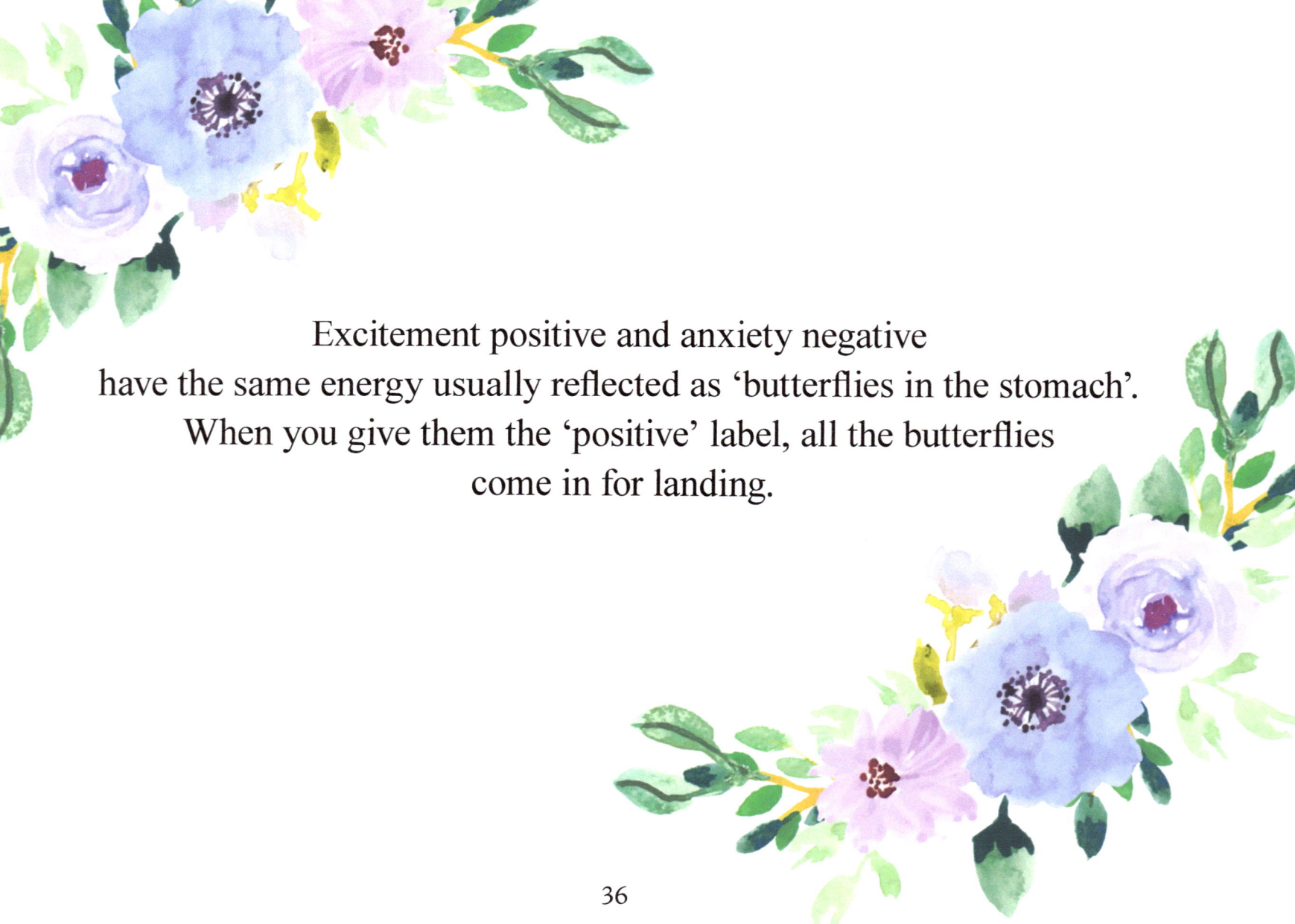

Excitement positive and anxiety negative
have the same energy usually reflected as 'butterflies in the stomach'.
When you give them the 'positive' label, all the butterflies
come in for landing.

What belief would you have to have
in order to create that particular reality?
What do you have to believe is true
in order to feel the way you do?

A belief is nothing more than a consideration.
A consideration is a thought – only possible because of the basic premise that you as a soul exist.

Behind all behaviour is a belief.
You cannot change behaviour without changing or letting go of the belief.

Believing is seeing. Not the other way round.

If you want to experience a different reality,
then change your viewpoint.
Change your belief.

If everything is perfect, there cannot be a right or wrong.
However, there is what is workable or what is unworkable.
Unworkable comes from beliefs that are held
but which do not serve you.

What belief would I have to hold
in order to experience the reality that I am experiencing?

Your beliefs create your behaviour, your actions,
your prejudices, your judgements and your assessment of self.
If your life is not going the way you wish,
examine your beliefs about life.

The intention, focus and concentration
for manifestation goes together with surrender and letting go.
After you have done this, your intention and the
Divine carry you along.

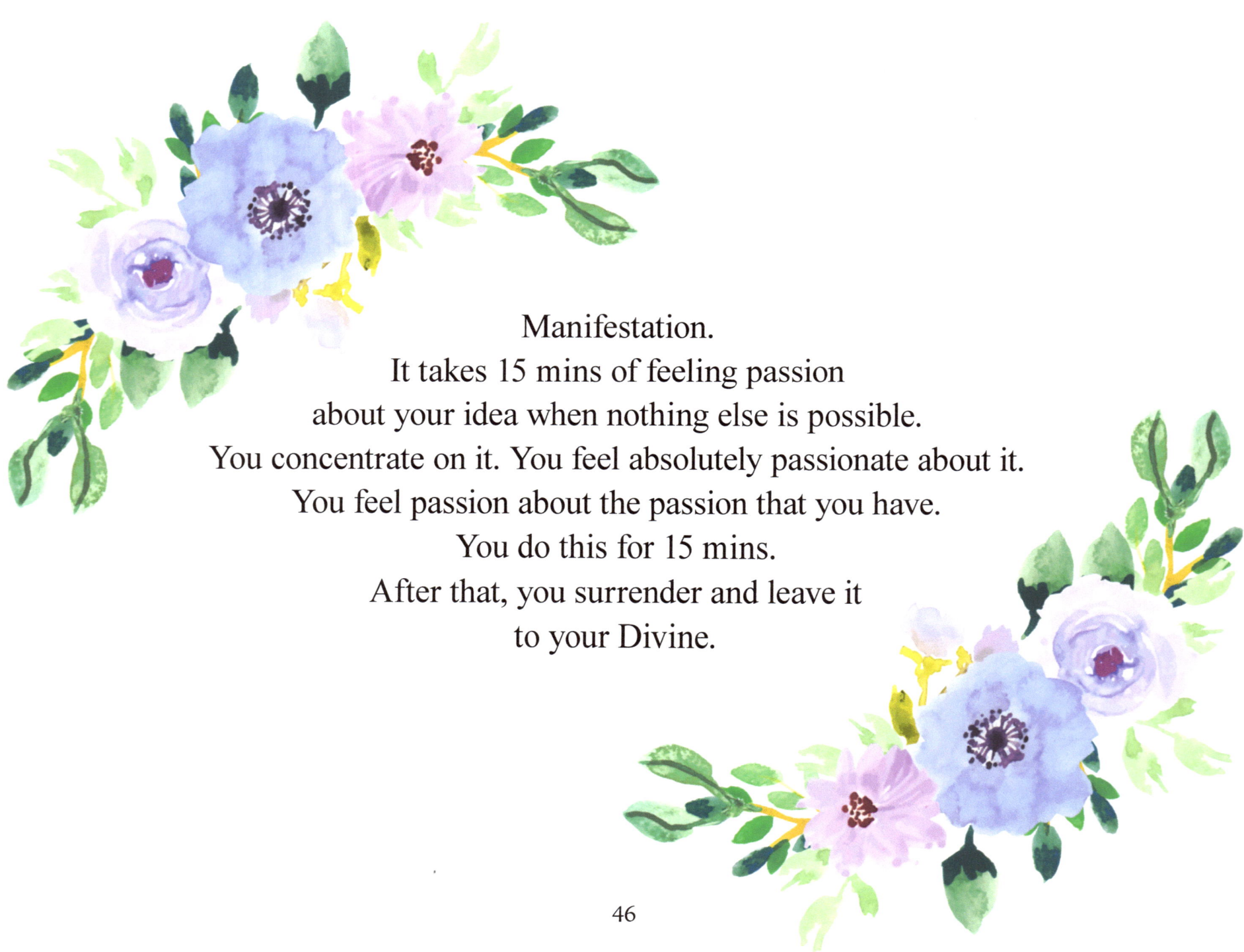

Manifestation.
It takes 15 mins of feeling passion
about your idea when nothing else is possible.
You concentrate on it. You feel absolutely passionate about it.
You feel passion about the passion that you have.
You do this for 15 mins.
After that, you surrender and leave it
to your Divine.

When you surrender, you also start to behave as though what you are manifesting is real.

Why not let your Divine take over
and assist in bringing about your desires:
those things that make you smile?

To love in spite of all
is the secret of greatness.
And may very well be
the greatest secret in this universe.

—*L Ron Hubbard*

Love is not blind.
Love lets the light in and everything seems brighter.

There is love.
Sometimes in a relationship, one does the loving
and the other allows themselves to be loved.

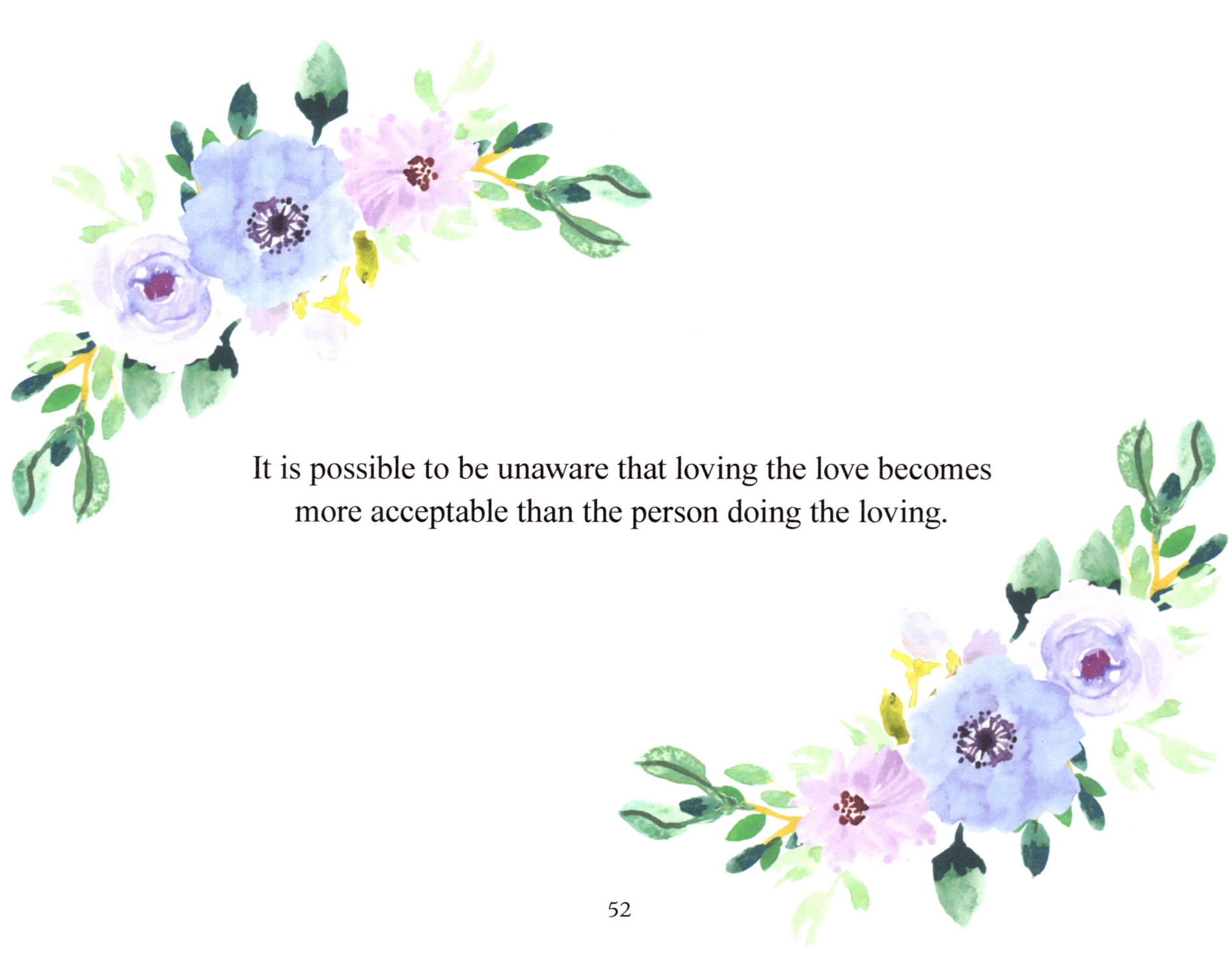

It is possible to be unaware that loving the love becomes more acceptable than the person doing the loving.

Hearts don't really break. They just stretch with exercise.

You cannot hate someone you do not love.
Love was the prerequisite basic emotion that made any alteration or any other emotion possible.

There is no balancing of merits.
There is just acceptance when real love is there.

Yesterday's hurt is today's understanding rewoven into tomorrow's love.

—*Walter Rinder*

You only feel left behind
if you were trying to catch up in the first place.

The only way someone can let you down
is if you considered they were holding you up
in the first place.

Marriage. Why marriage?
Because we need a witness to our life
to make it feel as though it was worth living.

You are the one you have been waiting for;
you are the one you have been looking for.

Why are you trying to fit in
when, in your own unique way, you were born to stand out?

Sometimes there is a need or even a passion to be right rather than be correct.

You can always agree that someone has a viewpoint.
You do not have to agree with the content.

Sympathy is an agreement that the other has been overwhelmed;
it is disempowering. Better to ask
"How could you or another handle this?"
Compassion is understanding.

She realised she had choices and that she never was trapped in any situation except by her own thoughts.

The word 'HOPE' implies despair;
Try substituting 'TRUST', a higher vibration that implies manifestation.

Audrey and Dr. Gordon also decided that one always had a choice of which attitude to adopt at the time and that they were only at the mercy of their own choices.

They had decided that response came
from responsibility; from realising that one's thoughts
and viewpoints were one's own internal choice.
Reaction came from deciding that an external source
was causing trauma and it couldn't be helped.

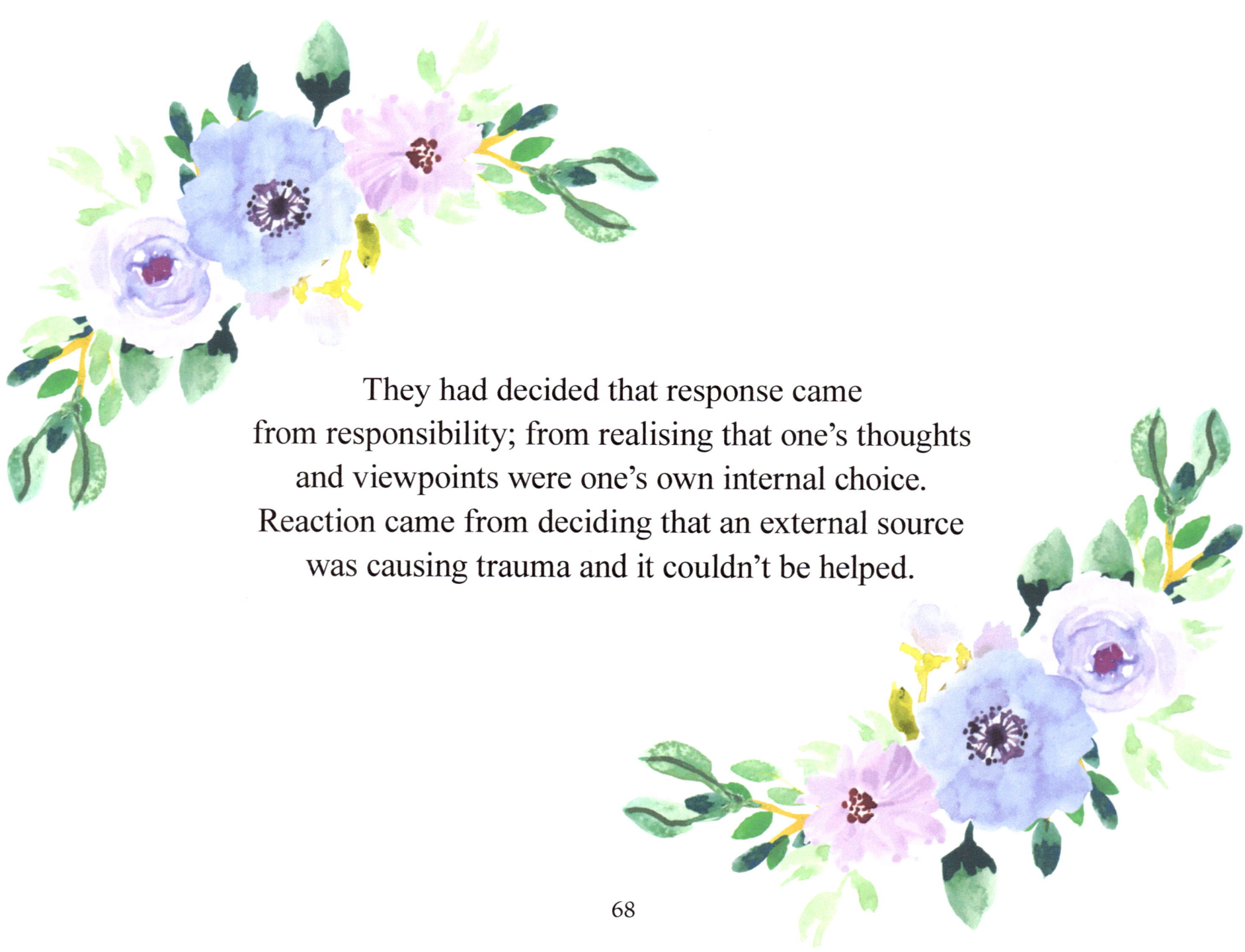

Responsibility does not mean blame, shame or regret.
It means to respond. Responsibility is the ability to respond.

You have to blame someone before you need to forgive them.

Unforgiving is very hard. It is unnatural and weighty.
Every time you look at the issue and don't end it by forgiving,
it places another weight on your shoulders
that you have to carry around.

I have to remember not to follow other people's ideas
no matter how well meaning they may be.

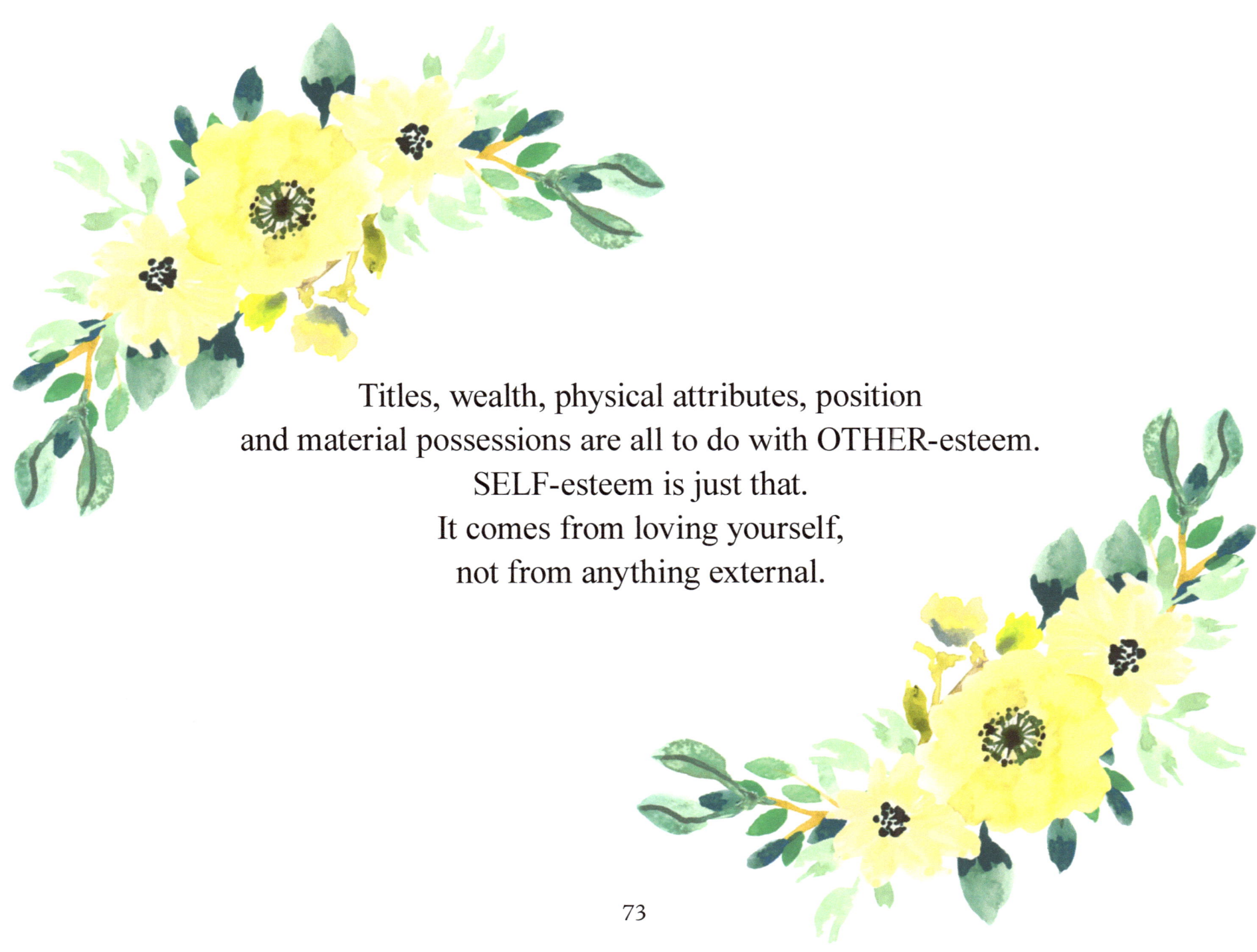

Titles, wealth, physical attributes, position
and material possessions are all to do with OTHER-esteem.
SELF-esteem is just that.
It comes from loving yourself,
not from anything external.

It takes tremendous (if unaware) effort to stay aberrated.
It is not a natural state for any being.

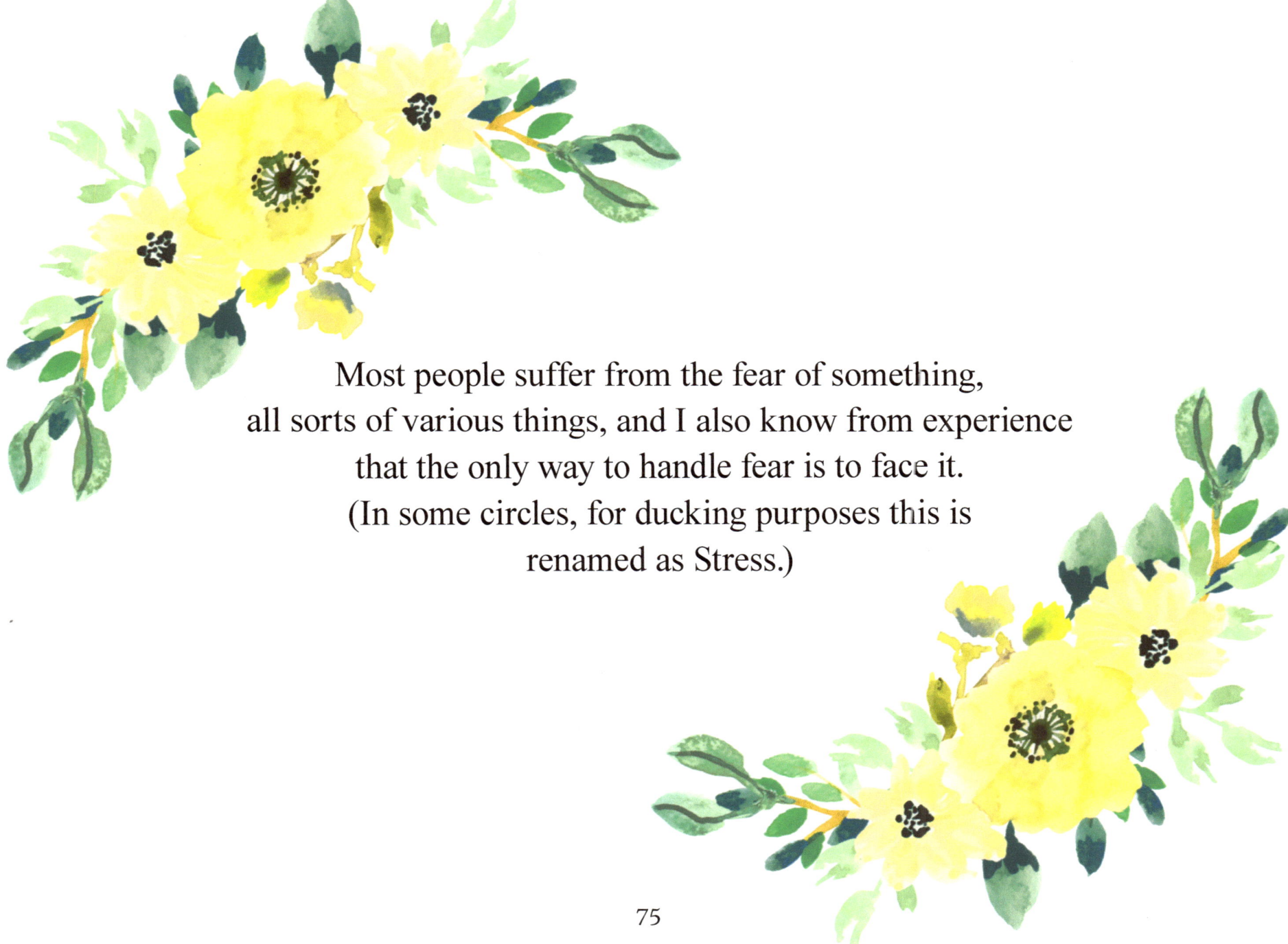

Most people suffer from the fear of something,
all sorts of various things, and I also know from experience
that the only way to handle fear is to face it.
(In some circles, for ducking purposes this is
renamed as Stress.)

You really need to do what you fear or to face it in some way.
This helps you to stay in present time.

Most people define fear by whether it is fair to themselves.

Suicide is basically a fear of living rather than a fear of dying.

When you have a book in your hands, you never feel alone.

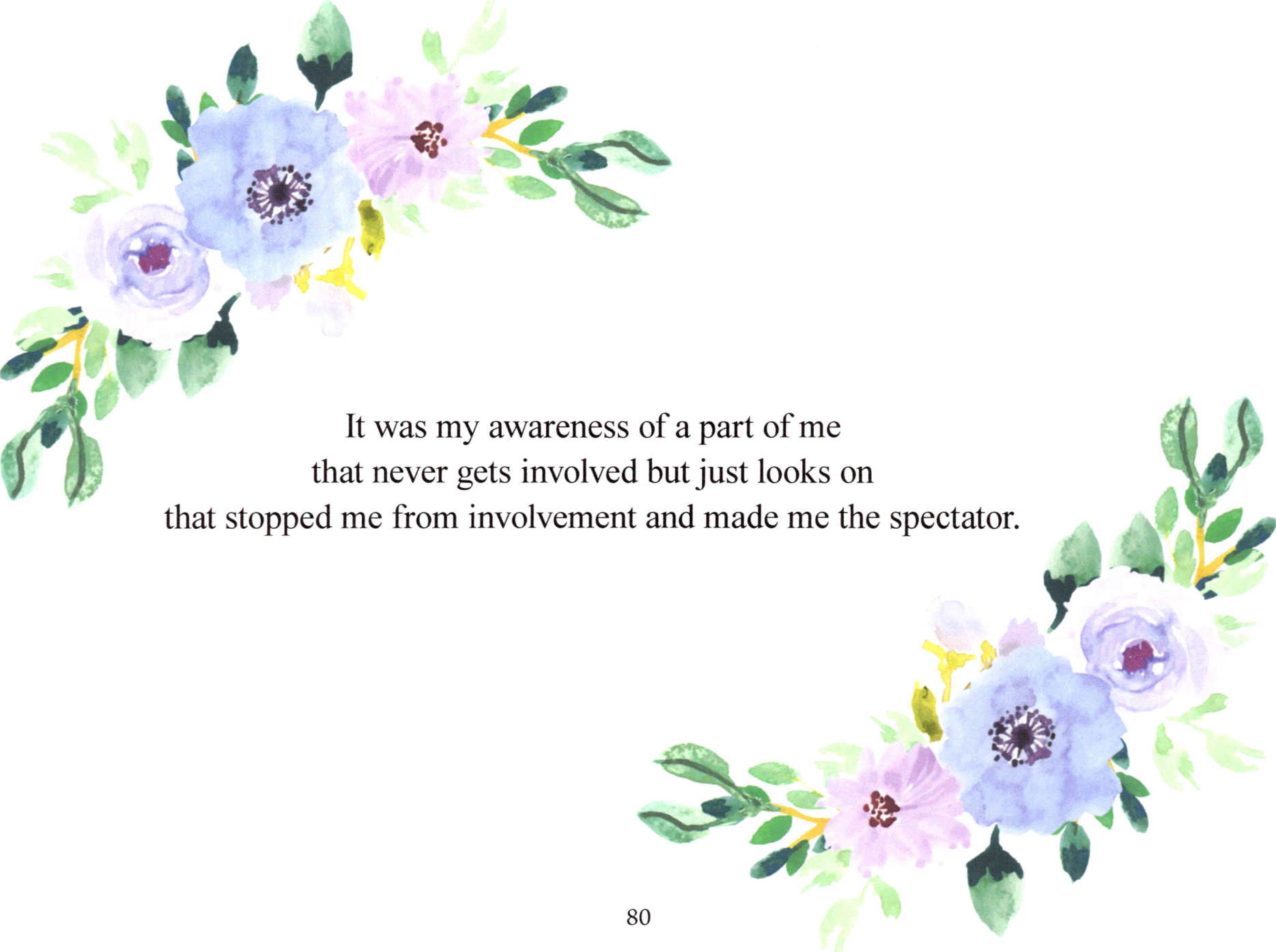

It was my awareness of a part of me
that never gets involved but just looks on
that stopped me from involvement and made me the spectator.

Perhaps I won because
it was alright to win or not to win.
Actually, I gave it no thought. I just enjoyed the game.
There was no desperation there or competitiveness.
Maybe that had something to do with it.

I only do things that make me smile.

If I'm going to do something, it will be done well;
It is an attitude that makes me smile, and as you know,
I've always followed that rule as much as I possibly can.

Data is not knowledge.
Knowledge and certainty come from applying that data.
Wisdom comes from living that knowledge.

Sometimes I just know things that I don't know I know and then it just happens.

Change. The evidence of life.

Everything is perfect just the way it is.
It always has been.

Jesus taught love.
Love is who you need to be: to be who you really are!

Jesus talked about love, compassion and understanding.
There is no judgement or limitation on real love.

Jesus taught love, compassion and understanding.
The rules, rituals, doctrines and judgement of most religions
have nothing to do with compassion and understanding.

If Jesus listened to the rules, regulations, rituals,
doctrines and judgement taught and often made as law
by all our man-made religions, he would be extremely mortified.
They have nothing to do with the compassion and
understanding that he taught.

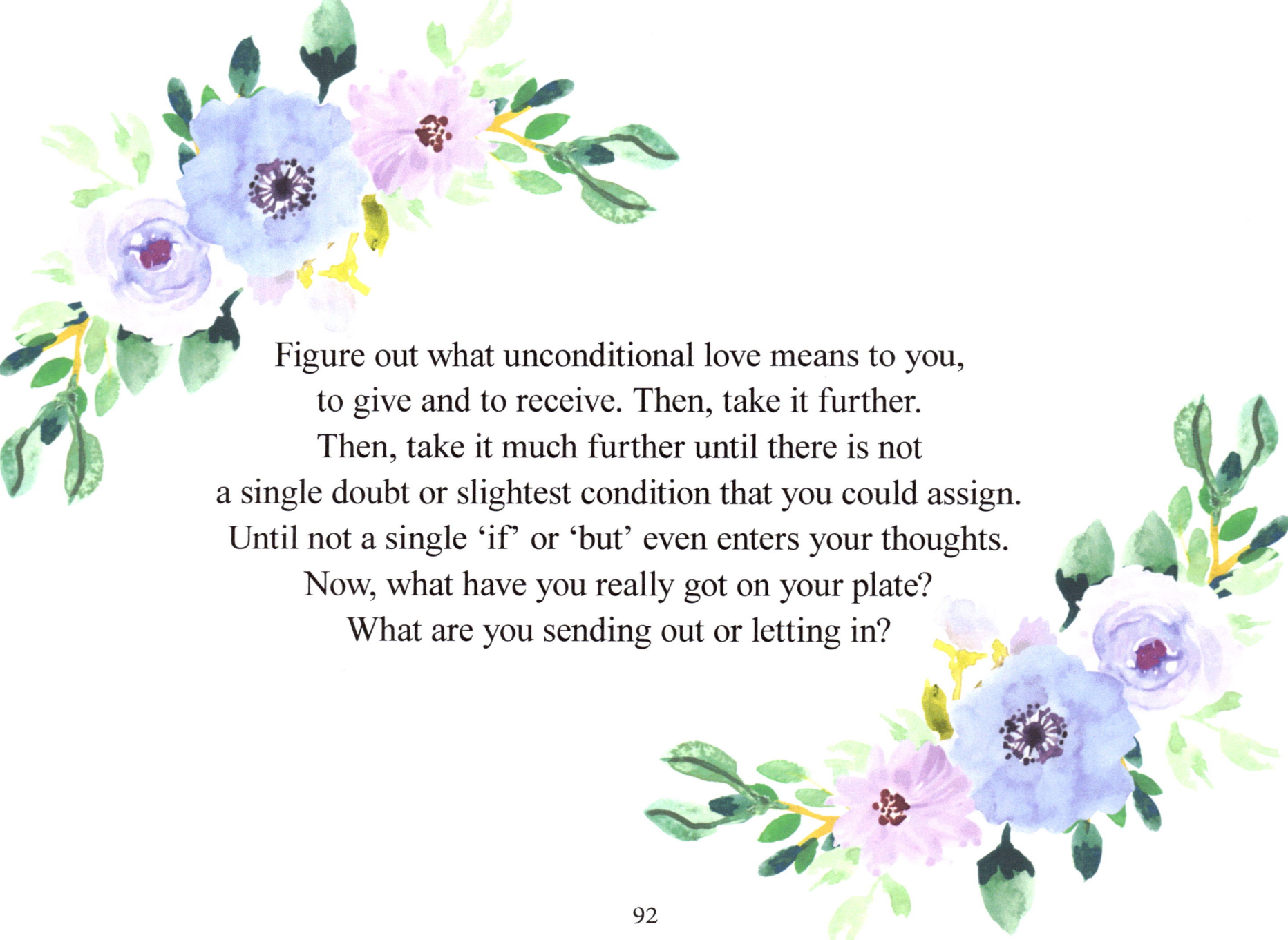

Figure out what unconditional love means to you,
to give and to receive. Then, take it further.
Then, take it much further until there is not
a single doubt or slightest condition that you could assign.
Until not a single 'if' or 'but' even enters your thoughts.
Now, what have you really got on your plate?
What are you sending out or letting in?

Even if your watch is broken, it is still right twice a day.

As a computer wizard, I make a very good cook.

Worry is like a rocking horse.
It gives you something to do but gets you nowhere.

Friendship. The delight and acceptance of another.

I should have been a bat.
Then I could have relished at being kept in the dark!

You cannot formulate a question
to which you do not already know the answer.

FOR THOSE LEFT BEHIND:

There is no life after death. There is only life after life.

Death (or dropping the body – a more accurate description)
is like walking into another room
with a much bigger window and a far better view.

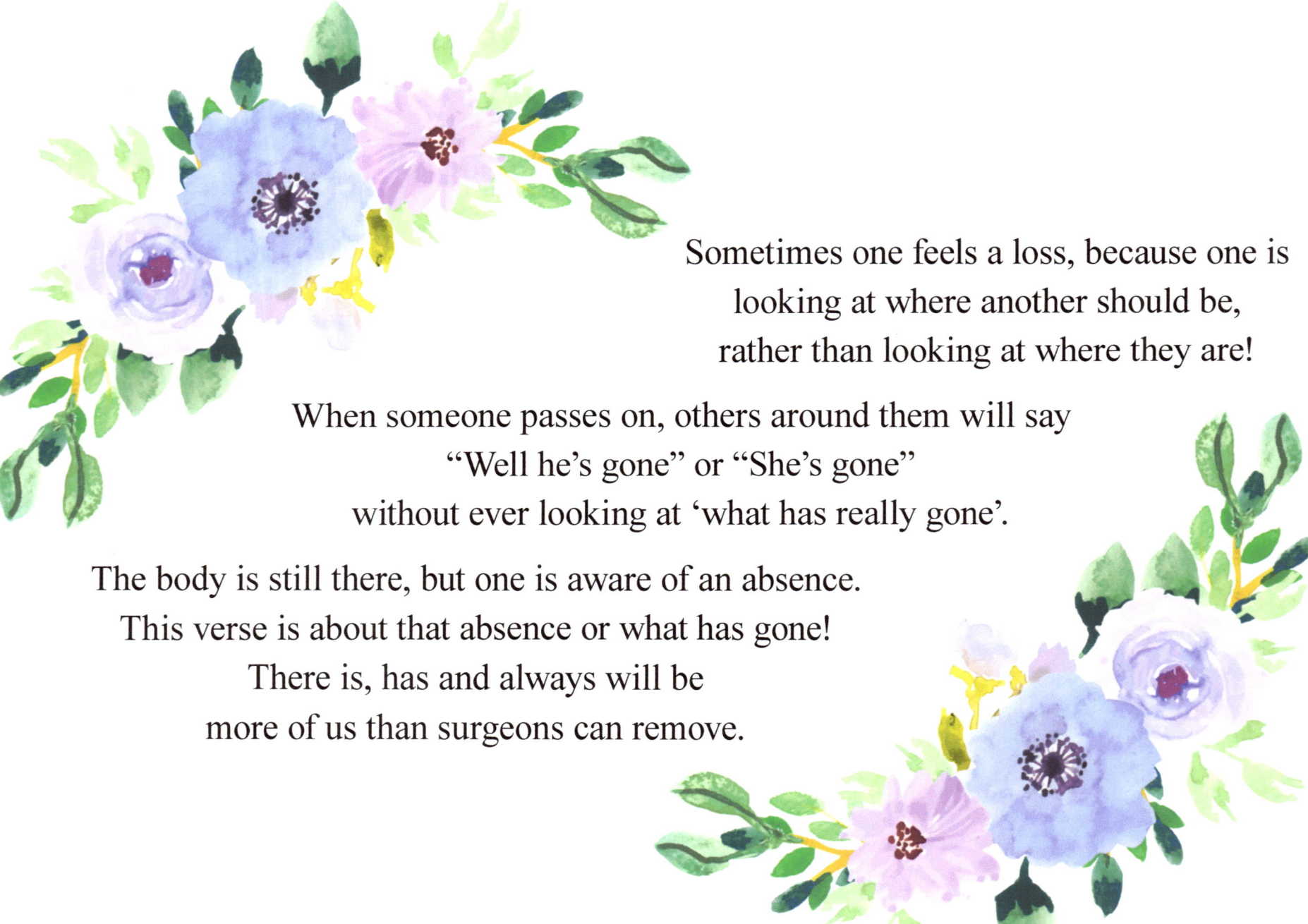

Sometimes one feels a loss, because one is
looking at where another should be,
rather than looking at where they are!

When someone passes on, others around them will say
"Well he's gone" or "She's gone"
without ever looking at 'what has really gone'.

The body is still there, but one is aware of an absence.
This verse is about that absence or what has gone!
There is, has and always will be
more of us than surgeons can remove.

People disappear but
they never really go away.
The spirits up there put the sun to bed,
stir up the moon; get the sun to shine and then
wake up the grass, the trees and the flowers.

They spin the earth in dizzy circles and sometimes
you can see them dancing in a cloud during the daytime
when they're supposed to be sleeping.

They paint the rainbows and also the sunsets,
make waves splash and tug at the tide.
They toss shooting stars and listen to wishes.

When they sing wind songs, they whisper to us,
"Don't miss me too much…
The view is lovely and I'm doing just fine."

OTHER TITLES BY AUDREY:

A Life of Enlightenment Volume 1

A Life of Enlightenment Volume 2

Audrey can be contacted at the details below:
Email: author@audreyo.com.au
Website: www.audreyo.com.au

Or alternatively you can contact
Audrey through her agent, Natalie Brown.
Email: agent@audreyo.com.au
Website: www.nataliejbrown.com

ABOUT THE AUTHOR

From the day she was born in England,
Audrey wasn't your typical baby girl – a characteristic
that has been constant to this day! Audrey started school at the tender age of three.
Grammar school followed at age ten.
She got engaged when she was only five and jilted her fiancé when she was eleven!
When she was fifteen, Audrey immigrated to Australia with her family
and continued to live an adventurous life
that would be considered unbelievable by most.

www.ingramcontent.com/pod-product-compliance
Lightning Source LLC
Chambersburg PA
CBHW050854010526
44107CB00048BA/1604